Profitable New Face Painting Business

Lee Lister is a Business Consultant with more than 25 year's consultancy experience for many household names. She is known as The Bid Manager or The Biz Guru.

From an early age she began an unparalleled journey through business consulting that continues to span across the UK, USA, Europe and Asia. She has consulted for many companies all over the world. Specialising in business change management, start up consultancy and trouble shooting. She is highly skilled in seminars, lectures and corporate presentations on business, project management and bid management. Lee's experience in marketing and internet marketing is also keenly sought after.

She is a prolific published writer of books, ebooks and articles on business, entrepreneurship and bid management. She can easily be found on major search engines and Amazon.

Profitable New Face Painting Business

Learn how to set up a profitable business, understand how to overcome the strains and stresses of a new company and become a Successful Entrepreneur.

www.ProfitableNewBusiness.com

Author: Lee Lister

Other books available include:

Entrepreneur's Apprentice

How Much Does It Cost To Start A Business?

Proposal Writing For Small Businesses

Profitable New T Shirt Printing Business

Start My New Cake Decorating Business

Start My New Manicurist Business

First published in Great Britain in 2009.

Published by: Biz Guru Ltd

Photo Copyright: © Paul Murphy

ISBN: 978-0-9563861-2-0

This book is dedicated to my daughter Kerry Lister for whom I have always strived to be my best.

Contents

Legal Notice

We do not believe in get rich quick schemes. We do believe that business is equal parts of inspiration, hard work and luck. We ensure that every book that we sell will be interesting and useful to our clients. Every effort has been made to accurately represent our product and it's potential. Any testimonials and examples used are not intended to represent the average purchaser and are not intended to guarantee that anyone will achieve the same or similar results

Please remember that each individual's success depends on his or her background, dedication, desire, and motivation. As with any business endeavour, there is an inherent risk of loss of capital. **There is no guarantee that you will earn any money**.

This book will provide you with a number of suggestions you can use to better guarantee your chances for success. **We do not and cannot guarantee any level of profits.**

This product is written with the warning that any and every business venture contains risks, and any number of alternatives. We do not suggest that any one way is the right way or that our suggestions are the only way. On the contrary, we advise that before investing any money in a business venture you seek counselling and help from a qualified accountant and/or attorney.

You read and use this book on the strict understanding that you alone are responsible for the success or failure of your business decisions relating to any information presented by our company Biz Guru Ltd.

Getting Your Business Started

Many people are thinking of starting a new business and face painting is certainly a popular choice. It is one of those businesses that you can start in a small way, providing you are able to obtain the necessary business licensing and certificates.

It is also a business that you can run quite easily from home with just a telephone and a simple filing system and obviously the appropriate equipment. You will need to ensure that you have a working room that is both clean and well equipped to a professional standard and some countries insist that you are regularly inspected.

It would also be advisable to have a background check if this is available. You should also obtain the appropriate insurance.

It would also be good to have at least two checkable references. Once you have all of these you should take photocopies and put them together as an sales pack.

If you have a good business plan, price your face paintings to make a profit and are good at time management, this can be a lucrative business.

Your main reason for wanting to start a face painting business should be that you are getting so many face painting orders that you feel you can go into business and make a go of it.

The Nasties

Tax, Insurance and Licences these are the nasties of your business and all of them are compulsory! Look up your local state/county/country web site to see what licences you will need. Similarly your country's tax web site will tell you what taxes you will need to pay, how you register to pay them and what forms you will need to fill in to become legal. Don't attempt to work without them – there goes the way to a world of misery. Tax officials in particular, are trained to find and collect unpaid taxes and these are always combined with extra costs and penalties.

Operating your business in some countries will require you and your staff to be licensed before you can start work. This should be displayed on your premises or available for view by your customers. You may also need a sales tax permit (USA and other sales tax based countries) or VAT registration (UK and some Europe and Asia) if you reach the VAT registration limit.

Will I Succeed?

You've got a great idea, you are pretty sure that what you have will sell; you've even got some cash together. Have you got what it will take to succeed? What else do you need?

Vision: You must be able to see where you are going and what the future will hold. See what others are not able to see and build your business on these visions.

Courage: The ability to act upon your vision despite having doubts. The readiness to give up job security and a planned future; for the chance of making a success with your new business. This takes courage.

Strategy: Having the courage to act upon your vision, you now need to build your strategies. You will need a business and a marketing strategy. These are the formulas that you will use to drive forward and manage your business.

Planning Skills: To ensure that you reach your vision, you need copious amounts of planning. Planning how you will reach your targets, how you will meet new changes and challenges and how you will improve your business. You will need a business plan and a marketing plan.

Researching: Having decided what your business is going to be, then you will need to find out who will want to buy from your business and at what price. This takes a fair amount of researching.

Conceptualising: Knowing what you want to sell and to whom, you now need to define your products and services. Brainstorm different things that you associate with your company. Include everything, good and bad, until you are out of ideas.

Keep in mind that ideas generate ideas. Write everything down, this is how you move your company forward.

Use this period to design your products, what you want your company to look like and how you want it to be perceived by your customers.

Creativity: You will need the ability to think outside of the box. Keep ahead of your competitors by coming up with new, unusual and unique concepts and solutions to their needs. You will need to create marketing materials, packaging and sales pitches – all will need verbal and visual creativity.

Determination: Along the way you will come across many hurdles and set backs, you will need to dig deep, make your changes and keep going. Determination and the belief in your visions and plans will keep you on the road to success.

Humour: When the entire world seems against you and all seems to be going wrong, when your customers seem to be your worst enemy then you need a sense of humour to carry you forward.

A Successful Business Start up

Right you have sorted out your business ideas, you are ready to go ahead and you know what you want to sell and to whom. Now you need your business structure. These are all the things that make up your business. They include:

- **Legal Base:** This includes such factors as your licenses, insurances and setting up your company.

- **Your Market:** You need to decide who you want to market your services to and where they will be.

- **Your Services:** You now need to decide what services you are going to offer to these people, how you would like to package them and what prices you wish to charge.

- **Your Business Plan:** Whether you are looking for funding or not – a business plan is the foundation of a new business.

- **Your Funding:** You should now take your business plan and look around for funding, starting with your Bank.

- **Your Premises:** Look around for your new premises, preferably in the middle of your potential market. Remember that central to your success is the position you choose for your business. Foot traffic past your door and many potential customers within a short journey from your new business is vital to you finding customers.

- **Web Site:** Most businesses have them now – so even if you don't want to set one up now – at least buy and hold onto your domain name – in case someone else gets hold of it.

- **Your Staff:** Good staff that reflect your business ideals are vital so spend some time spend some time finding the best staff you can.

- **Marketing:** So important and so difficult to get right. Start with a good marketing strategy and go from there.

- **Grand Opening:** Make sure you make a splash and attract as much curiosity as possible.

Your Business Framework

When starting a business of what ever kind, large or small, there is a always a require framework or scaffolding that you have to set up. Not only does this make your business much more effective, but it also saves you from a lot of embarrassing and costly problems. When you start up your business, remember to tick off the 10 items below and you will have a very sound start to your business. Here is your framework:

– **Business Name.** Choose an appropriate name that sums up what your business stands for. It has to be unique – try and ensure that a suitable domain name is also available as you will probably want a web site as well. The owner of an established web site might cause problems if you give your brick based business the same name – so be careful in your choice.

- **Your Business Entity.** Obtain professional advice as whether to the best way to set up your business as a limited company, partnership etc. Then register your company.

- **Patents and Trademarks.** If you have unique products then you need to ensure that you have registered your patents before your start trading. Similarly any product names, mottos, selling tags etc should be trademarked. Take professional advice on how to do this.

- **Licenses and Permits.** Ensure that you have all the licenses and permits that you are legally required to have.

- **Insurance.** You may think that you don't need this but you do and will. So take out property, business, vehicle liability, staff and disaster insurance. A good broker can advise you.

- **Taxes.** A necessary evil I am afraid. Register with your local tax collector. Set up a good accounting system and hire a good accountant.

- **Employment Laws.** Establish what you local employment laws are and ensure that you adhere to them. Set up employee guidelines and handbooks. Make sure you hire and fire legally.

– **Banking.** Visit your local banks and find the best business bank account and credit card for you business. Always keep your business and personal spending separate.

– **Business Plan.** This is your carefully written plan on how you want your company to operate, what you want to sell, where and to whom. It includes your business and marketing strategy as well as your financial standing and projections. This is the foundation of your business.

– **Liquid Cash.** Ensure that you have enough money to carry your through the first few months of your business as well as any foreseeable troublesome times ahead.

How Much Does It Cost To Start A Business?

You've got your business idea, think that you will be able to get a good loan and even have your business plan being written but.... The one big burning issue is – How much does it cost to start a business?

Well you first of all have to be realistic and understand that you are unlikely to make a profit within the first six months of business – so you should also budget for your first six months running costs. So here is your shopping list:

1) **Purchase of lease/franchise/premises.** This will include any Realtor fees, deposits and other legal expenses. Even party sellers need some kind of premises. To start with you can use a home office, but you are going to need somewhere to hold all that stock and marketing materials that you will soon need.

2) **Cost of fit out and purchase of new equipment.** This will include any work that needs to be done on your premises as well as any equipment you have to buy in order to start and run your business. Often you can lease equipment in order to mitigate high start up costs. This also includes a car or van to deliver your stock to your distributors.

3) **Six months worth of advertising and marketing.** This will be particularly high at the start as you establish your business. Factor in some cold calling as well as a launch party or opening day. Marketing will include a lot of local advertising in order to attract good distributors.

4) Legal, licensing and banking costs. Your business will need to be set up correctly, licensed and have a good bank account. Sadly all of these require money. You may also need a payment processing service to use credit cards.

5) **Staff costs for six months.** Staff will be the basis of providing good service to your new customers. Make sure that you have enough money put aside to find them, train them and keep them! Much of your staff costs will be on a commission basis but you will still require admin staff. They will all want to be paid, often before you get paid for your sales.

6) **Uniforms, office and marketing supplies, packaging etc.** You will need to establish your brand. This means that your staff will need uniforms or at the least business cards and name tags. You will need brochures, adverts etc. Your office will also need office equipment and supplies. You should also budget for designing your logo, brochures and adverts if you cannot do this yourself.

7) **Stock and supplies** – to keep you going for six months.

8) **Maintenance for six months** – your equipment will also need to keep going for six months. This includes your cars, computers, printers, copiers etc. Budget for a lot of printing ink!

9) **Any loans that you have will also have to be paid.** Again look at least at six months or until you break even and can pay the loan.

10) **Your salary for six months** – lastly you will need to pay your own bills and maintain your family during this time. You should expect that for a short while your standard of living will go down.

Add this up and add 10% for contingency and some good luck.

Common Business Mistakes.

All entrepreneurs have to learn from their own mistakes as they build their business, but wouldn't it be great to have some one tell you what the common mistakes are and how to avoid them? You Want a Successful Business – So Don't Do This!

- **Believing that you will start earning straight away.** All businesses take time to establish themselves – even internet based ones. People need to know where you are, what you sell and most importantly, that they can trust your company to deliver what it promises. Expect to spend at least 6 months working away at your business before you break even – sometimes longer.

- **Believing that you can set up a business and it continually earns for you.** Even a very profitable business needs continual management to ensure that your profit does not erode. Your products and marketing need to continually change to meet the changing circumstances in the real world.

- **Believing that you can earn whilst you are aware from the office.** Even if you fully automate your business and hire really good staff, there is always an element of "while the cat is away". That is why there are so many "absent owner" sales.

- **Being a single product company.** As good as your product may be, markets and tastes will change and so must you. If your product is very good – other companies will quickly take action to seize your market share by bringing in similar products at cheaper prices.

- **Not offering upgrades and enhancements.** It is far easier and cheaper to sell to existing customers. You do this by offering upgrades and enhancements to their existing products. You should have a group of products at several increasing price points.

- **Relaxing after you success.** Businesses need continual effort, management and improvements. Although a product launch is hard work, you should start on your next product shortly afterwards. This will give you sustainable success and several income streams.

- **Believing that a business can be established with little capital.** Marketing, infrastructure purchases, stock, advertising and staff all cost money and must be purchased in order to make a profit. Cash flow kills more business than anything else.

- **Believing that you know all you have to**. Your competitors may have been in the business longer than you have, your customers may be very knowledgeable. Meeting customer needs is a constantly changing landscape and you need to keep up to date on the latest trends and technology. You need to be able to project yourself as an expert in the field you work in. If you do not have this knowledge then learn it or buy it in!

- **Not investing in your staff.** Your staff are the public face of your business. They should be well trained, knowledgeable and well dressed as well as fully motivated to sell on your behalf.

- **Believing in Get Rich Quick Schemes:** A good business is established by part inspiration, part perspiration and just a little bit of luck!

- **Not motivating** your staff. Good staff are hard to find and difficult to keep. Good staff help your business expand and be profitable. Good staff will grow your business exponentially as word of mouth spreads so you must look after them or you may find them working directly for your client.

- **Not motivating** your distributors or sales staff sufficiently. Selling on commission only is very hard work, it must be rewarding and your staff should feel that they will benefit from it. Your distributors, particularly at the beginning will be chasing around looking for retail outlets, doing a lot of mileage, delivering stock and looking after retailers. So they need motivating and reward well.

– **Geographic problems.** Once you get established, the geographic area you are selling to becomes larger. Care must be taken that you can get to your new customers. The cost of travelling must be properly calculated and included in the sales price.

– **Stock Holdings.** With distribution problems come stock holding problems, the more products you have, the more stock you must have. If you have different sizes and colours this figure goes up even more! It is very important that you work out how much stock you need as stock is dead money hold no more and no less!

– **Branding.** It is important that your company is recognised and has a good image. This helps spread the word about your services! Otherwise why would your customers hire you? Spend on your brand, it's worth it!

Learn these lessons well, avoid the mistakes at all costs you should save valuable time and resources by doing things right the first time.

General Face Painting or Specialising

There are many types of face painting. You might want to be a generalist or you might want to specialise in one kind of face painting or one style. Some ideas you might want to look at are:

- General face painting for all that require it. Using a booth, stall etc.
- School or club face painting – going from club to club or school to school.
- Mobile face painting – going to boot fairs, clubs etc. as you can get bookings.
- Parties and celebrations – you can align yourself with party planners or wedding planners and become one of the acts or entertainers.
- Celebration days – specialise in Halloween, Christmas, and Easter etc.

You might also look at different styles of face painting, such as pets, fantasy, super heroes, butterflies etc.

To be general gets you a potentially bigger audience, but niche selling gets you more loyalty from your customers and the potential to be remembered more.

Painting Other Bits

Face painters don't just have to paint the face. Cheek painting is also popular, lot least because it is quicker and easier. Full body painting is popular with some people and you could find a nice little niche with your local theatres or movie stages! Maybe you can start a trend with feet or hand painting. Lastly look at painting baby bulges for mothers to be!

Safety Cautions When Face Paintings

F ace paintings are a great opportunity to start a business but it is also something that requires safety. Like anything else, when doing face paintings you have a responsibility to take some safety precautions to not make your face paintings pose a safety hazard to anyone. Many people who do face paintings do not realize the safety steps that are not only used in selecting paints, but also in other materials that you can use in undertaking face paintings. You must also know how to properly clean your tools that you use to create face paintings and things you need to do to protect yourself form some possible problems. Here is a quick reference to these safety tips to help you create a safe environment when doing face paintings.

There are many types of paints to use in face paintings, but not all of them are safe. The only type of paints you want to use in your face paintings are skin safe paints.

It does not matter if it says natural, non-toxic, chemical free, or any other reference to being chemical safe. Chemical safe does not mean that the paint was designed or tested for skin use.

If you use any types of glitter, then you need to use only FDA/BHA approved glitter for cosmetic purposes. This type of glitter fits the safety and types of substances that are safe to use for the face.

When you clean your brushes and any other equipment that you use for face painting, only use water to clean them. If you use chemical agents, then there could still be residue left from the chemical that can pose a safety hazard when using it the next time.

One very important tip when face painting is to not paint on anyone who has sensitive skin, has abrasions or injuries to the face, or who even has acne problems that can turn into open wounds.

These types of skin situations can lead to some serious repercussions. To be safe, it is better to not take a risk and avoid face painting in these types of situations.

Obviously you need to clean your brush between customers as well as change any pads you might use. This not only looks professional buy ensures that germs are not transferred from one customer to another.

The most important aspect of face painting is to protect yourself. Always make sure that you have your body in a comfortable position at all times. Many people do not realize that you can seriously sustain an injury from face panting.

This can happen due to continually keeping your body in different positions, as well as bending your body, arms, wrists and hands back and forth. Always be sure to make sure that your body is not becoming to tense and be sure to take some small stretching breaks to relieve your body's tension.

By following these safety precautions when face painting, you will not only have a safer environment, but you will also have less problems. These simple face painting tips will protect you and the people you do face paintings on.

Getting Your Face Painting Designs

If you have been face painting for some time then you will already have some favourite designs. However to keep fresh and popular you will need to keep updating the designs that you use. You can find them in:

- Books - comic books, art drawing books, animal books, toy books and catalogues.
- The internet or the library.
- Art supply stores, especially in kits.
- New stencils being sold.
- TV, movies and book heroes and cartoons.
- On eBay and similar you can buy CD/DVD's of art work that you can turn into designs.
- Colouring books, cake decorations, embroidery designs etc.

Keep up to date with the children's world, try out the designs on paper first and keep upgrading your skills.

Some simple ideas for face painting young children are: Flowers, bunny, sailboat, turtle, spider, duck, butterfly, ladybug, dinosaurs, ghosts, cross, puppy, bear, kitty, fish, alien, dolphin, fruit with faces, facial expressions, names, flags, clowns, feathers, birds, street signs.

You may want to include sparkles, pastel colours, glitter gel or rubber stamps and stencils, and stick-on jewellery to accent your art work.

If you want something more simple and quick to apply, try temporary tattoos. Although not your own personal artwork, these are still a form of art, and there are loads of them on the market. All you need to apply these is a bowl of water and a face towel.

A silly and fun idea is to paint a fingerprint of a parent on a child's face, using the person's own finger, of course.

Maybe for laughter, you could even paint a toe print of a child on a parent's face. Paint the name of a favourite pet on a kids face.

A mom at home could try dipping a willing pet's paw into the paint and stamping it onto the kid's face. For quick fun, try face painting stamps. Draw a picture of a face onto a big piece of paper and have the child stamp a design on the face using a special face stamps.

The ideas for kids face painting are limited only to the imagination. When painting faces of a younger child, you must have patience, allow time for possible fidgeting, and keep your design simple. It helps perfect your talent to practice the chosen designs in advance of an event. Most children would be happy to cooperate in being a guinea pig for your practice sessions.

Your Start Up Needs

There are a few things that you will need on your start up. These will make you look professional and help you market your business.

Your Sales pack

The sales packet is the major step in the face painting business – it is what makes your business professional. The sales packet must contain a printout or photocopy of your terms and conditions, insurance and background check, references and your brochure.

In your terms and conditions you should explain the details of your working policy. This will give information such as: your hours of operation; when a deposit and full payment is due; if you will deliver or not etc.

All these details should be included in your terms and conditions in order to not only look organised and professional but also to avoid misunderstandings in the future.

Your Brochure

Your brochure can be quickly made up on a PC. Design a one page description of your business and the kind of work that you do. Include your contact details and company name. Do not include too many words – just make it catchy, memorable and informative. You can include a couple of graphics which you can easily find on the internet.

If you wish you can also include a business card. These can be professionally produced from web sites such as vistaprint or from you local stationary store or printer. Now you have your sales pack.

Your Uniform

It would also be a good idea to give yourself some kind of uniform. You can buy smart coveralls from large department stores or uniform stores or you get t shirts or sweaters printed with your company name. Visit CafePress for some ideas.

Match your colours of your uniform and your equipment to your company colours. This makes you look like a professional company.

Items You Will Need

Face Painting is a relatively cheap business to start up but your will need a few items. Most supplies for face painting include water based paints for easy removal. The problem sometimes with the face paint is the quality of the product. Hot weather can be an enemy as the perspiration can ruin the artwork or cause the person being painted to perspire while you are trying to apply the paint. So ensure that you buy as good as quality as you can afford.

You will also need to invest in the proper, good quality brushes. Detail brushes are sold as low as £3 each. A brush can make a big difference in the finished quality of your work. If you purchase a cheap brush with an end that is too big or frays or scatters easily, you could be sorely disappointed in the outcome and having to fight the brush to get the effect you desire.

Profitable New Face Painting Business

Theme sets are a popular choice for face painting. Used especially at Halloween, these are sold with instructions to achieve whole face outcomes.

A person can enjoy becoming like a lion, monster, pirate, mermaid, ghost, cat, mouse, favourite cartoon character, and much more.

Some stores sell rubber stamps in their supplies for face painting. The stamps are created with an impression and simple designs to make fill-in work quick and easy. They have foam backing for easier use. The cost is about £8 each and the size is 2 inches by 2 inches.

Some face painting kits are sold for as little as £4 a kit. These would be fine for children to use for play or for beginning artists to use just for practice or fun. They provide a low-cost option for charity events, such as school fundraisers or church functions where the overhead must be kept low.

Profitable New Face Painting Business

Some kits are sold with 6 face paint pencils, a sharpener, sponge, and white face paint for a base colour. For the more advanced artists, stencils are sold at prices ranging from £20 to £45; including a video. These are used with airbrushing, which has become a more popular form of face painting. Glitter gels and stick-on jewellery can be added to accent your artwork.

You also could buy a piece of poster board or cardstock to show your available choices for purchase when setting up your booth. Maybe you'll want to invest in a carry-all, chair, and small folding table as well.

In your office you will need:

- **PC and printer** for research, pattern making and business administration.
- **Idea board** to post ideas torn from magazines.

Equipment List

Equipment List	√
PC	
Colour Printer – laser or inkjet	
Design Software	
CD/DVD's of designs	
Face paint	
Uniform and/or apron	
Towels	
Tissues	
Bowl for washing	
Paper for invoices, receipts, correspondence, marketing etc.	
Sales Pack	
Branded labels	
Sales Pack	
Business Cards	
Brochures and flyers	
Message board	
Accountancy package	
MsOffice	
Email account	

Starting Small With Your Premises

Sometimes circumstances dictate that you can't afford a retail shop but you really want to get your business started. Many small, retail businesses are not suitable to run from your home base or via a warehouse. Web sites, whilst having low start up costs, also take a lot of marketing and time to become profitable. Why not think about starting a kart or kiosk in a shopping mall? Here are a few points to consider.

Mall Karts and Kiosks

As always Location, Location, Location: The location of your business is crucial to its survival. A store's location can often spell its success or failure. Without sufficient store recognition, a business can suffer poor cash flow and will inevitably fail over time. Your business needs to be physically located out in midst of everyday life, in broad daylight where shoppers can easily find you.

The location itself of the mall plays a huge role in your kart's success. Is the mall located in an isolated part of the city or town, or right in the heart of the action? You must forecast the level as well as the timing of traffic your business will receive during the morning, midday, and late afternoon on each day of the week. Therefore, you can efficiently establish an employment schedule as well as appropriate operating hours.

Choose your mall carefully so that it has ample traffic of potential customers. Go there with a "clicker" and see how many people pass by per hour. Visit on several different days of the week as well as at different times.

Quality of Traffic: It is one thing to have steady traffic, and another to have the kind of traffic that your business needs. Some malls attract low-to-middle income people; others are targeted towards the upper class. Choose wisely.

Position in the Mall: Your success in a mall will depend on whether you are located in a section that is conducive to what your business is selling. You should look at the **complementary nature of the adjacent stores.** If you are a gourmet store, you may want to be located near a restaurant where people are already in their "hunger fulfilling" state of mind. Complementary businesses, such as fine jewellery and gourmet food, have also been proven to work well together as both its customers are likely to have disposable income and a tendency to spend for these two genres of luxury products.

Similarly **high volume areas** where lines of patrons form, such as theatres or department stores, are also good mall locations as it could give potential customers several minutes to look in your display or listen to your sales pitch.

Costs: Rental costs in shopping malls are often higher than rates in downtown Main Street. You main consideration should be: will the higher traffic compensate for the increased rental cost?

If you can easily recover your monthly rental payment and overhead expenses, you're in a good position to make a profit.

People Buy with their Eyes! Lastly ensure that you display your products in an tempting manner. Karts and Kiosks are very good in selling items that are "impulse buys". Make your products appealing and your sales pitch interesting and your sales will increase!

Lastly, as business improves, you can easily buy or lease another kart!

Market Stalls and Boot Fairs

The same criterion about location appertains to market stalls and boot fairs. Obviously your outlay will be much smaller – but so will your potential income. Care should be taken to ensure that your stall looks professional and well branded otherwise your business will be classed as a "hobby business" and people will expect to pay correspondingly low prices.

Street Painting

If you have the appropriate permissions you can set up your stall in a busy shopping precinct or mall. Busy parents often want to keep their young children amused on a busy shopping trip. Christmas and Easter would be a particularly good time.

Clubs and Schools

You can also negotiate to be a regular at schools and clubs. Visiting every two months or so. You could match this with a talk or a story if you have these skills.

The Mobile Face Painter

Some face painters make money by going to the event. If course you will need a robust carrier box for your equipment, a couple of comfortable folding chairs, a table for your kit and cloths and water to clean up. You should also invest in a lock up box for your money.

Kids of high school ages have enjoyed having their faces painted at pep rallies. They have been painted with their mascot paws, team logos or names, school names and colours on their faces for fun and for fundraising. It's an easy way to earn money for the senior class or an upcoming class trip.

Set up your booth at local arts and crafts shows, midnight madness sales, and during special school functions. Low prices keep the student customers coming back or persuade them to purchase more than one picture.

Profitable New Face Painting Business

Face painting has been used as a way to earn money for special needs, such as a charity event.

Idea for places to do kids face painting include: shopping malls, hospitals, birthday parties, charity events, festivals, school events, flea markets, church functions, craft shows, parades, open house events, zoos, parks etc.

Hobby stores may offer classes for kids face painting or might allow you to offer classes yourself. They may be interested in allowing you to set up in order to draw more business and delight their younger shoppers who accompany the parents or relatives.

How about setting up outside your sports arena and painting faces in the club colours? Decide upon a quick and attractive design, get there early and get the appropriate permits and you should be ok.

Pricing Your Product

Pricing is so important to the success of your business. When pricing your face painting look at the following:

- Cost of the materials.
- Travel costs to the face painting.
- A percentage of your equipment costs.
- Cost of your time actually face painting.
- Booth, kart or stand costs.

You should set some money aside to build up your brand image by advertising and training your staff. People are more likely to come to you if they know your product.

Now have a look at what other face painters are charging and try and ensure your prices are similar.

By managing your stock levels to an optimum level, you should be able to keep the costs to a minimum.

Two valuable lessons to learn are:

- Limit the amount of conversation between you and the participant during the actual painting and learn to control your brush. If you make the child giggle, you may have to start all over when your brush strays and smears paint in an unwanted area.

- Make a picture chart of the drawings and colours you are able to offer. Know how long each drawing takes, what materials it needs and what each design costs. You can then set each design into a price category.

Check List For Starting A New Business

You are ready to give up your job to start your new business, or even scarier, sink your savings into your new business. You just want to make sure that you have done everything possible to succeed, here is a check list for you.

1. Legal Stuff:

–Do you have a memorable business name and the associated domain name?

–Do you have a legal name and business entity?

–Have you got all your licences?

–Have you got all you certificates such as health and fire?

–Have you registered everything you need to?

–Have you told the tax department and got your numbers and details?

–Are all your shares, statutory meetings etc correct?

–Do you have all the patents and trademarks you need?

–Do you have the legal documents on your premises – leases, sales, mortgages etc.?

–Do you have all the posters and legal manuals etc that you need?

2. Strategies and Planning:

–Do you have your Business Plan written?

–Do you have a Business Strategy?

–Do you have a Marketing Strategy?

–Have you decided upon what Business Model you will use?

3. Protection:

–Do you have your insurances for you, the company, liabilities, staff, premises and vehicles?

–Have you got health insurance for you and staff if necessary?

–Do you have your pension set up?

4. Finances:

–Are your finances in place and have you signed all the forms necessary?

–Do you have enough and on the right terms?

–Have you got your bank set up?

–Do you have your credit/debit card and payment processor set up?

5. Premises:

–Are your premises/office ready and equipped?

–Are all the utilities that you need connected – gas, electric, phone, broadband etc.?

–Do you have all the vehicles, computers and machinery that you need?

6. Staff:

–Do you have all the staff you need?

–Are they trained or ready to be trained?

–Do you have the necessary uniforms?

Your Unique Selling Point

You've heard about a Unique Selling Point and guess that you want one but you have no idea what it is and why you need one. Often called the U.S.P – it means – "What makes your company, product and services different from all the other companies selling the same thing?

Now obviously in a crowded business environment – be it click or brick – you want your company to not only stand out but be memorable. You USP will do this for you.

So how do I define my USP?

Have a look at you company and a few companies that you believe compete with you. Also look at a couple of companies who are trading as you would wish to trade in the next few years. For products we mean products, goods or services.

So, what product features could you have that would make you different from your competitors?

–Look at what products you sell the most often or most of.

–How do these products differ from each other?

–What benefits do these products provide?

–What better features do you/ you could provide?

–What features do competitor's products have that yours do not?

–What features do your products have that are different you're your competitors?

Make yourself stand out from your competitors and emphasise this in all your fully branded marketing materials and you should not only stand out from others but also look larger, more professional and memorable.

Branding, The How's, What's And Why's

Your business brand says a lot about you and your business. If you create a strong brand image, it will elevate you above your peers and provide a good model for your product and service development as well as a sound foundation from which to expand your business.

What is Branding?

Many people think that having a logo and maybe a short description of their services is all they need to set up their brand. This is not so.

Your brand encompasses all that your business does, from first contact with your potential customers through to how your products are defined and sold. Your brand is what defines and describes your business. Look at any two different companies that compete in the same market and look at how people recognize and remember them.

For example look at Rolls Royce and Toyota - they both sell cars but each company is known for a different reason. Someone looking for a car on a budget would not go to Rolls Royce - yet both sell their cars on reliability. Clearly more people would aspire to purchase a Rolls Royce, but many also be happy to purchase a Toyota.

Look again at the perceived value of a brand. Why is the iPod the desired MP3 product when other brands have similar properties and reliabilities? People perceive the ipod to be superior and are willing to pay more for the pleasure of owning one. Indeed many people would not consider any other purchase. This is clever branding by Apple who marketed their product as being very desirable to certain markets.

I Don't Have that Kind of Money.

So Why do I Need to Create my Own Brand?

The main reason has to be to differentiate yourself. You are starting a business in a very crowded market so you need to stand out from the hobby workers and other competitors.

Branding also makes the promotion of your company and development of your products so much easier. There are thousands of new businesses and many times more web sites. You need to:

–Set yourself apart from the competition

–Make yourself memorable so that people will either look for your business or choose you above your competitors.

–When introducing your business to a new customer, your brand should go before you and communicate much of what you want to say.

Your Face Painting Designs will be easier to define if you centre them around your brand definition. For example if you are selling fantasy designs your brand image will be totally different than if you are selling children's character designs You need to appeal to a different market – i.e. young adults as opposed to young children and their parents.

So How Do I Create My Own Brand Then?

You brand must say:

- Who you are.
- What you do.
- How you do it.
- What the benefits of using your business are.

You brand MUST establish your company and build your credibility with your prospective customers.

In order to be able to do this you must first be able to describe what you want your business and products say, so start with your Mission Statement or Elevator Statement.

- **The Mission Statement** - this is what you want your business to be or do as it operates. You need to be realistic and focused. Being profitable is not a mission statement, but deciding what you want to do to be profitable is.

- **The Elevator Statement** - This is 1-4 sentences that you would use to describe your business, in the time that it takes to travel in an elevator - or a few minutes. It is used when meeting new people who ask "and what do you do?" or as an introduction when networking.

What Should Be Described Within My Brand?

First of all, pretend that you are one of your target customers and list 5 things that they will be seeking from your product. These items would encompass a short definition of one of more of the following:

–Price.

–Quality.

–Service.

–Support.

–Scarcity or availability.

–How and when delivered.

–Accessibility.

–Security.

So now define who, what and where you are in these terms and you should come up with something like this as a Mission Statement.

"We will provide quality fantasy T shirts to Suburbia. We will include fairies, dragons, Goths, monsters and unicorns and have the widest selection we possible can."

Your elevator pitch might be something like this: "We provide quality character based face designs to children via our parties and market stall."

Tag Line

Now need to be recognised by your customers. Here is where you tag line and logo come into play.

My tag line - what's that.

Well if you become as well known as Nike it can be something very short like "Just Do It" - but that is a few years and few £million down the road. Your tag line is a short description of what you do.

Something like "Face designs for sports clubs and their fans" which explains what you sell and to whom. It also differentiates you from other companies in your area.

Logo's

Now you need a logo - it does not need repeating that this should also reflect your brand. If you are saying you are modern and efficient - you don't want an old fashioned, messy looking logo. It should always reflect your brand and be simple and recognizable.

You should include it on:

- –All your communications.
- –Your web site.
- –Your products.
- –Your packaging.
- –Your marketing and promotional materials.
- –Your adverts.

Working with your brand

Your brand is so much more than your logo; it is your company name, your web site and the colours that you use.

Remember your brand allows you to pre-sell your company and products as well as ease the introduction of new products as you become more established. Be consistent with your brand promotion - don't keep changing it as people are more likely to remember things the more they see them.

Regular marketing enables you to establish your credibility and relevance to your target market.

Branding, Correspondence And Other Stuff

Branding is so important. It is how people recognise your company and what you are selling. Everything that your customers and staff see should be "stamped" with your company brand and be instantly recognised as belonging to your company. Let us look at where your will be using your brand

Business Name

Pick a great business name that reflects the type of T shirts you are selling and who you are selling to. If you are getting a domain name (and you should, even if you don't want a web site just yet) you need to match this with your company name.

Invoices and Order Forms

It stands to reason that all your correspondence, including that used in delivering your proposals, order forms and invoices, should be stamped with your company name, logo, phone number and web site.

Marketing Material

Once again you should market such that your company and how to contact it, is instantly recognisable. How and where you advertise should also back up your brand image. If you are selling family friendly items then you would not advertise in a "lad's mag" for example.

Your brand is so much more than your logo; it is your company name, your web site and the colours that you use. Everything that your customers and staff see should be "stamped" with your company brand and be instantly recognised as belonging to your company. So let us look at where your will be using your brand.

Website, store, kart, market stall

However you sell your services they must have your logo and contact details emblazoned over them as well as completely reflecting your brand.

Marketing Your Business

The first thing you need to do is contact your friends and neighbours and see if they need your services or know someone who does.

Now set up an advert on your PC. You can print them off, on postcards quite easily. It should read something like this.

---

face painting

face paintings for births, celebrations and weddings

For more details,

Call CompanyX: 123-4567 - ABC face paintings

In essence, you have a professional advertising "billboard." Now is the time to use a bit of shoe leather.

Put the cards on notice boards in supermarkets, shops, clubs, offices etc. Always ask first. You can also put a similar advert in your local papers if that is affordable.

If you also decided to use business cards – use the front to put your company name, contact details and a one line description of your services. On the back put your short advert. Leave these wherever you are allowed to and concentrate on where you will find your potential clients.

It takes a short while to start up any kind of company. Start touting for small contracts to begin with particularly those that you can do yourself. As you get more work or get offered larger contracts you can start to consider taking on staff.

Sales packs

Set up an sales pack. It should be quite small – say A4 or A5 and a few pages. It will include details of your company and products as well as a few sample designs, your prices and some great photos of face paintings you have done. Include some references if you have them. This will be given to prospective customers who are seeking to purchase bespoke or customised face paintings.

Onsite Marketing

Whichever retail outlook you chose, ensure that you have plenty of brochures available to give out to interested potential customers. Don't leave them on the counter otherwise you will go through a lot of them for little return – save them for the really interested people. You could leave business cards for anyone to take- people tend to take these only if they are interested. You should display some good samples as well as a lot of items for sale. Be prepared to take orders from your stall.

Administration

Administration is very important. Without good administration your company will quickly disintegrate into chaos and you won't know who has what and who needs to pay for services and who needs them to be cleaned and when. Your administration should include ways of controlling or managing the following:

- Collecting money from your customers
- Banking money.
- Managing enquiries and complaints.
- Invoice and bill payment.
- Accounts and book keeping including, payroll, banking, taxes and VAT/taxes.
- Purchasing and auditing equipment. At least once a year and preferably quarterly, equipment must be checked against your accounts and for the need to be repaired.
- Salary and commission payments.
- Staff training and development.

It may seem a lot, but if you start small and get yourself a good accounts package, a good accountant and bank manager it is a lot easier.

Customer Administration

– Set up a file for each of your customers with their contact details, what you have agreed to do, the price to be charged and any other details. Keep a folder/file for each customer. Add each order to the file – latest order on top. The file should include all contact details. If you have a number of orders per client put a list of orders on top and tick them off as you complete them. If you have a lot of customers have a customer number format.

– You should also keep a record of money due and paid. You should be able to find a good accounting system very easily. Always give a receipt.

– Make a To-Do list of all your orders and tick off those that have been completed. Put in order of importance/when delivered.

- Keep a detailed diary of when you have to be where. In the diary also note what extra services were requested and what payment you need for the service.

- Keep a diary of what money is due when and by who – refer to it each day and chase that money! Keep invoices separate to use for your accounts and to keep track of what you are owed.

Your Customers

Once you spread the word that you're in the business of face painting you'll have no trouble at all keeping busy!

When prospective clients call or email you, explain your services and prices. With this kind of service it is best to either ask for a 50% deposit or a 100% payment. This is because once you have finished the service; it is sometimes hard to obtain the payment due. Make sure that you receive all the payment due before you finish the service.

First Contact

When a prospective customer calls, have your appointment book and a pen handy. Be friendly and enthusiastic. Explain what you do and offer to show a few samples.

When they ask how much you charge, simply give them a wide range and say that you will give a firm cost quote, once you've discussed their requirements.

Then without much of a pause, ask if 4:30 this afternoon would be convenient for them, or if 5:30 would be better. You must pointedly ask if they can come to make your cost proposal at a certain time, or the decision may be put off, and you may come up with a "no sale." You may prefer to visit them if you do not have a suitable reception area.

Just as soon as you have an agreement on the time and place to make you cost proposal and marked it in your appointment book, ask for their name, address and telephone number.

Jot this information down on a 3 by 5 card, along with the date and the notation: Prospective Customer. Then you file this card in a permanent card file. Save these cards, because there are literally hundreds of ways to turn this prospect file into real cash, once you've accumulated a sizeable number of names, addresses and phone numbers.

Estimating

When you go to see your prospect in person, always be on time. A couple of minutes early won't hurt you, but a few minutes late will definitely be detrimental to your closing the sale. If they are coming to you then ensure that you give good directions and are ready for them.

Always be well groomed. Dress as a successful business owner. Be confident and sure of yourself; be knowledgeable about what you can do as well as understanding of the prospect's needs and wants. Do not smoke, even if invited by the prospect, and never accept a drink - even coffee - until after you have a signed contract in your briefcase. It's important to appear methodical, thorough and professional

A little small talk after the sale is appropriate, but becoming too friendly is not. You create an impression, and preserve it, by maintaining a business-like relation ship.

When you go to make your cost estimate, take along a ruled tablet on a clipboard a calculator, your appointment book and your list of sample designs.

You should also have at least two of your sales packs (one for the customer and the rest for her friends that may also need your services) and a blank contract (more of this later). A receipt book would also be a good idea. You can buy folios in stationary stores that will keep these all tidy.

If they choose one of your sample designs, fine, but if they want a particular design of their own, now is the time to ask for photos or start jotting down all their requirements, including sizes and colours.

You should hopefully come up with a drawing of what they require in front of them. Get them to sign off these details and picture so that there is no dispute later. You will probably have to come back to them with a firm price.

Make sure that it is possible for you to actually produce this face painting!

Discuss when they need the face painting and if you are delivering the face painting of if they are collecting it from you.

Now complete the contract for them, summarizing what you have just agreed and confirm that you will send her a typed up list of all the face painting decoration details you have just completed. Ask them for confirmation on the contract and for a deposit if applicable. Also offer them an sales pack for their friend who may need your services.

Congratulations you have just made a sale!

Putting Your Business On The Internet

Just about anyone can put a web site up on the internet and now days it is quite easy. You have two choices as how to set up your website:

- As a shop window for your company, with contact details etc.
- As a fully working site with ecommerce facilities.

Which ever option you choose, you first need a god domain name. Go to a good domain provider like enom, Godaddy, namecheap NOT registerfly and spend under £10 on a domain. Choose a domain name that has the word dating, love etc in it. This will help with your search engine positioning as well as act as a memory jog to your potential customers.

As A Shop Window

Hop over to hostgator or similar and then buy a monthly hosting account. With that will come a site maker - where you can easily set up a web site using one of thousands of templates. You can add payment processor linkages, forums etc.

The only problem you will have is you want to sell promote or talk about illegal activities, terrorist activities or sex or have a high usage activity such as MySpace etc.

As A Full Site

You will probably need to get this especially written and designed for you. Put your project on sites like guru/elance/scriptlance etc and find a competitive quote.

Get yourself a PayPal account or similar so that you can take payment on your web site. This is much more secure and quicker than taking checks.

Factors To Remember

Always consider your target market when designing your web site. Include some helpful information about your subject matter but nothing that will give away what you are trying to sell!

Ensure that your contact details can be freely found and that details of your company and services are clearly set out.

As you will be asking for money before you deliver something – make your potential customer feel comfortable making payment and tell them what will happen next.

Respond to all enquiries and purchases very quickly. If this is difficult then set up an autoresponder to confirm you have received their enquiry/payment and will get back to them within a few hours.

Place references that you have received from past customers to show that you are a professional company.

Your challenge will be to be listed in the major search engines and then get traffic. Now market your web site like mad. It will take several months to make an impact in the major search engines. So build up your local custom whilst you

are doing this. www.GetIntoGoogleFast.com –
Does exactly what is says in the domain!

An Internet Marketing Strategy

Ok, you've got your web site set up, you are sure that it is search engine friendly and you are pretty certain what your customers want. You've identified at least 3 products that you want to promote and you think that they meet your potential customer's needs. So now what?

Well unfortunately the days, that I can remember, of "build it and they will come" have long gone. Unless you promote your web site – no one will know that you are there and no visitors means no sales.

So, take a deep breath, a pen and paper and let's start on your Marketing Strategy. Briefly for a new business, with a relatively inexperienced marketer, your strategy will probably include the following options:

– Pay Per Click Advertising

– Article Marketing

– Email Marketing

– Community Marketing

– Classified Advertising

So let's get started – and before you start panicking, you are just writing your Marketing Strategy. This chapter will explain how to do all of the following.

Internet Advertising Kit

For each of your programs/products

- Write a short advert – say 50 words.
- Write a very short advert – say 15 words
- Write a short article – say about 400 – 600 words.
- Decide on your keywords – say about 30 – 50 words.

Internet Marketing Kit

For your web site theme

- Write at least 6 short auto responder messages.
- Find or write at least 2 giveaway products.

Internet Marketing Tools

- Your web site
- An autoresponder
- A good email account

Internet Marketing Strategy

Now let's put all of these together into your first Marketing Strategy.

1. **Submit your web site to all the major search engines.** This will start to get your web site noticed. As this takes a long time, it needs to be the first thing that you do. You can do this yourself or pay someone else to do this for you. We provide this service for our customers for £20 a month, which includes submission to Google, Yahoo and MSN.

2. **Set up your download pages**, for your bonus products as well as the products you are selling. Ensure that you provide an extra offer on each download page.

3. **Set up your autoresponder form** on your web site and load your messages into the autoresponder. Ensure that you offer one of the giveaway products as a bonus for signing onto your ezine. The second giveaway can be set up for message 3 or 4. Your messages should be sent in the following intervals. Day 1,3,7,7,7,7

4. **Submit your article** – including your resource box, to about 6 major ezine article sites. Limit yourself to 6 at the moment. Each of these submissions, if accepted will give you a link to your web site. If too many links to your new web site appear very quickly, search engines assume that you have been using "black hat" SEO tactics (a total no no) and will not list your site.

5. **Identify 4 forums** that discuss the topics of your web site. Set yourself up an account name that describes you well. We use the name "Biz Guru" which is our trade mark and name. Set up your signature to include your web site address. You now have 4 good links to your web site.

6. **Answer Questions:** Start answering questions asked within the forums. Do NOT post adverts for your web site or products. Use this time to establish your credentials. If you answer questions well and contribute to the forums, your web site tag will be noticed.

7. **Set up a PPC campaign** – you can start with the smaller search engines first. Take your very small advert and your keywords and use them in your campaign. Most search engines will help you with your choice of keywords. Remember to set a budget and test, test and test again until you get quality and converting traffic.

8. **Set up some classified ads**. You can do this one of two ways: i) choose one or two major sites/email lists and advertise with them. ii) use an ezine ad blaster to send your ad out to numerous lower quality places.

9. **Test, Update and Modify**. Review, change and add to your PPC keywords. Submit more articles and adverts. Start tactfully promoting your products in the forums.

Well that's what to do to be a success. Good Luck.

Expanding

Expansion means growth, involving people working for you, more jobs to sell, and greater profits. Don't let it frighten you, for you have gained experience by starting gradually. After all - your aim in starting a business of your own was to make money, wasn't it? And expanding means more helpers so you don't have to work your self to death!

Staff

So, just as soon as you possibly can, recruit and hire other people to do the work for you. The first people you hire should be people to handle the basic work that you do..

You can obtain good staff by word of mouth, advertising in your local Job Centre, supermarket etc. Look in your local university and local school and ask amongst friends.

You will find a lot of people who want to work part time here which you will need at the start of your business.

You can start these people at minimum wage or a bit above, and train them to complete every job assignment in two hours or less. You might consider hiring people on a contract basis so that if they don't work you don't pay. You don't get loyalty here though.

You should also outfit them in a kind of uniform with your company name on the back of their blouses or shirts. A good idea would be to have magnetic signs made for your company and services. Place these signs on the sides of the cars your people use for transportation to each job, and later on, the sides of your company vehicles.

Advertising

A good supply of business cards wouldn't be a bad idea for them either, in order to advertise your services to others they come in contact with. The only other form of advertising you should go with would be a display ad in the yellow pages of your telephone directory. As you get larger you can investigate advertising in local magazines.

Extras

You might also want to expand by offering story telling and children's parties with your face painting. You could also look at becoming a face painter for local sports clubs etc.

Customer Contracts

When you're dealing with customers, sometimes things can go wrong. It might be your fault, it might be their fault or it might be no-one's fault -- but if you didn't make a contract, then you'll all suffer.

Why Do I Need Contracts?

A contract gives you a sound legal base for your business, and some guarantee that you're going to get paid for your work without you having to ask the customer for payment in advance. In the event of a dispute, the contract lays down what the agreement was so that you can point to it and say what was agreed. If you ever end up having to go to court (let's hope you won't), the contract is what the judge's decision will be based on.

Without a contract, you leave yourself vulnerable and open to exploitation.

Someone could claim that the terms they agreed with you were different to what you say they were or that they never signed up for anything at all and so they won't pay.

It's especially common to see big businesses mistreat small ones, thinking that they won't have the knowledge or the money to do anything about it. Essentially, contracts take away your customers' ability to hold non-payment over your head, and give you the ability to hold it over theirs instead.

Written and Verbal Contracts

It is important to point out the distinction in the law between a verbal (spoken) contract and a proper, written one. A verbal contract is binding in theory, but in practice can be very hard to prove. A written contract, on the other hand, is rock-solid proof of what you're saying.

You might think that you're never going to get into a dispute with your customers, but it's all too common to find yourself in a little disagreement.

They will often want to get you to do some 'small' amount of extra work to finish the job or make it better; not realizing that doing so would completely obliterate your profit margin.

For this reason, you should be very wary of doing anything with nothing but a verbal contract. On the other hand, if you were incautious or too trusting and only got a verbal contract, it could still go some way towards helping you, especially if there were witnesses.

Won't It Be Expensive?

Written contracts don't necessarily need to be formal contracts, which are drawn up by a lawyer with 'contract' written at the top and signed by both parties.

These kinds of contracts are the most effective, but can be expensive to have produced, not to mention intimidating to customers.

The most common kind of written contract, oddly enough, is a simple letter.

If you send a customer a letter laying out your agreement before you start work, and they write back to agree to it, that is enough to qualify as a written contract, with most of the protections it affords. It is best to get confirmation from your customer that they have received this contract.

If you are doing high-value work for some clients, though, it could be worth the time and trouble of having your lawyer write a formal contract, or at least of doing it yourself and getting a lawyer to look it over.

Formal contracts will give you more protection if the worst happens, and there's nothing to stop you from making it a one-off expense only by re-using the same contract for multiple customers. PLEASE: TAKE PROFESSIOANAL ADVICE.

Contracts for Small Purchases.

Obviously it would be silly to expect everyone who buys some £10 product or service from you to sign a contract, or write back indicating their agreement to your terms. In this situation, you should have a statement of the 'terms and conditions' that your customer is agreeing to by buying from you, and they should have to tick some kind of box indicating their agreement before you send anything.

The Top 5 First-Year Mistakes

Even once you've got past the starting-up stage, there are still plenty mistakes to be made, and most of them are going to be made in your make-or-break year -- the first one. Here are the top five things to avoid.

Waiting for Customers to Come to You

Too many people wait for their customers to phone, or come to the door, or whatever. They get one or two customers through luck, but nothing like enough to even begin paying their costs. These people sit around, looking at their competitors doing lots of business, and wonder what they're doing wrong.

You can't be like this. You have to go out there and actively try to find customers. Talk to people, call them, meet with them -- whatever you do, don't just sit there!

Spending Too Much on Advertising

So everyone tells you that the only way to get ahead in business is to advertise. Well, that's true, but you need to make sure that you stick to inexpensive advertising methods when you're starting out. Spending hundreds of dollars for an ad in the local newspaper might turn out to get you very few new customers, and you will have spent your entire advertising budget on it.

Make your money go further with leaflets, direct mail or email -- these are easily targetable campaign methods with high response rates and low costs. Remember that it is always better to spend money on an offer than on an ad, and always better to spend money on an ad than on a delivery method.

Being Too Nice

When you're running your own business, it can be tempting to be everyone's friend, giving discounts at the drop of a hat and making sure that you don't hassle or inconvenience anyone.

That's all well and good, until you find that your Good Samaritan act has just halved your profit margin without lowering the cost to the customer by very much at all.

Sometimes, you need to realize that you've got to be harsh to make a profit. Give people discounts to encourage them to buy or to come back, not because you like them or feel sorry for them. Don't be afraid to be ruthless in your pursuit of business success. Nice guys don't finish last, but they are running in a different race -- one with much less prize money. If that doesn't bother you, of course, then feel free to go for it.

Not Using the Phone

You'd be surprised just how common phone fears are -- if you're scared of the phone, you're not alone by any means. Many people are terrified of making phone calls, and avoid them wherever possible. I have seen more than one business owner reduced to tears on the phone and trying desperately to hide it from the customer.

You need to try your best to overcome your fears, as talking to customers on the phone is almost as good as meeting them for real. Letters and emails are useless by comparison.

The best way to overcome phone fears varies from person to person, but it can often be as simple as making the phone fun, by calling friends and relatives often for a while and getting used to it. Alternatively, try working in telemarketing for a while -- if that doesn't make normal phone use look like a walk in the park by comparison, then nothing will.

Hiring Professionals for Everything

It can be tempting to think that, since you're starting out, you should just find a company or person to do every little thing you need. People seem to especially overspend on design services.

You might think it'd be great to have fancy graphics all over your website, but would it really increase sales? If I saw it, it would put me right off. Likewise, a slick brochure often fails to say anything more than 'I'm going to charge you a premium to pay for my expensive brochures'. Don't hire someone unless you can demonstrate that the service they're going to provide will increase your profits by more than the amount you're spending -- if you're not sure, try it yourself first, and you can always upgrade it later.

Problems You May Have

As in any business you will get problems, sometimes just knowing what you may face is a great help.

- Some customers use office email to correspond with you. Make sure that you are discrete with the headings used on the emails to them.

- Some customers are never satisfied. Just make any reasonable changes that are requested. Be polite and patient.

- Some customers may have problems explaining what they want – this is where your product sheet comes in handy. Make sure that you write down everything that they request and get this agreed to.

- Some customers are very slow in replying – ensure that you give them a time limit to reply and then send two further reminders – telling them when the last one is.

Time for a Holiday: But How?

When you've been working long and hard at your business for a while, you might feel like you've earned yourself a little break. There are business owners out there who haven't taken a real holiday since they started their business -- including some who started their business as long as five years ago!

After all, how can you ever just desert your business and your customers and go bronze yourself on the beach? How can you avoid being on call 24/7 throughout your holiday? Well, everyone deserves some time to themselves at least once a year, if they want to keep being productive and avoid stress. Here's what to do.

Tell People When You Are Going Away.

You can't just disappear when you're running a business -- you need to let people know long in advance that you're not going to be available, and make sure that they have everything they need to manage without you while you're away.

It's best to schedule your holiday not to interfere too much with the business.

However much you might want to have your holiday in the summer, it's important to remember that every business has its quiet months, and you should schedule your holiday in the period where they seem to be.

Change Your Voicemail Message.

A quick and simple way to let people know that you've gone away is to change your voicemail message.

This allows you to still hear what people have to say when you get back, and stops them from wondering why you never seem to answer your phone.

A good format for the message is as follows: 'Hi, this is [your name] at [company name]. I'm sorry I'm not in the office right now, but I will be back on [give a date]. If you leave a message, I will be sure to get back to you'.

If you work from home don't give a coming back date unless you want to invite the local thief into your home!

Set Up an Email Auto responder.

Similar to a voicemail message, but less commonly used, is the email auto responder. Again, you don't want people to wonder why their emails are going unanswered, so your best bet is to set up your email program to automatically reply to any email you get with a message saying that you've gone away.

Example: 'Hello, and thank you for your email. This is an auto responder, as I'm away on holiday until [date]. I have received your email, however, and will respond to it upon my return. I apologies for any inconvenience to you, and I am willing to make an offer of 10% off your next order to make it up to you.' The special offer for people who get the auto responder is a nice touch -- it makes them feel lucky that they emailed you while you were away, instead of frustrated.

Don't Stay Away Too Long.

Of course, when you go on holiday, you're relying on people being willing to wait for you. That means you can't really take the kids to Disney World for two weeks, or spend a month staying with a friend abroad -- it's just too long to be away from your business for.

You should regard a weekend away as ideal (it avoids the whole problem for the most part), and a week as the maximum you can allow yourself. Don't let people make you feel bad about only taking one-week holidays: after all, you could always have more than one each year.

Alternatively: Get Someone to Look after the Business.

If you really want to get away for longer, or it's essential that your customers don't have any break in service, then you could consider getting someone to look after your business.

This could be an existing member of staff that you make your 'deputy', to be in charge while you're away, or it could be someone who's related to you and has some experience running a business. You could even hand the business over to a competitor that you're friendly with and share the profits with them, if you think they're trustworthy and they could handle it. Enjoy your holiday!

In Conclusion

One of the most important aspects of this business is asking for, and allowing your customers to refer other prospects to you. All of this happens, of course, as a result of your giving fast, dependable service. You might even set up a promotional notice on the back of your business card (to be left as each job is completed) offering five dollars off their next bill when they refer you to a new prospect.

This is definitely a high profit business, requiring only an investment of time and organisation on your part to get started. With a low investment, little or no over head requirement, and no experience needed, this is an ideal business opportunity with a growth curve that accelerates at an unprecedented rate. Think about it. If it appeals to you, set up your own plan of operations and go for it! The profit potential for an owner of this type of business is outstanding! Good Luck.

Index

Profitable New Face Painting Business

Lightning Source UK Ltd.
Milton Keynes UK
UKOW052029060812

197135UK00002B/176/P